A Glass for Love, Hate, and the Perpetual Party

Scott R.S. Raphael

Dedicated to:
Gia

Table of Contents

A Glass for Love, Hate, and the Perpetual Party

Prelude: The Perpetual Party

Entry

I thought that I was looking through glass.
I stepped and then I fell.
And as the air went shooting past,
I thought, "it's just as well."

A Glass for Love, Hate, and the Perpetual Party

It's a party, can't you tell?
Alone at the bar,
(a glass in your hand)
(thoughts of a seedy one-night stand)
(a grand invitation to your car);
to meet
(ripped leather seats,)
(she cheats, you cheat,)
under aluminum sheets,
all a perversion of your head,
an inversion of the dread
simmering, designing,
unabashedly pining
for the immersion of the dead
(the insertion of lead in the
back of the nape)
(draping your face in linen)
and left within
until the spasm
of an unwelcome orgasm
sparks you back awake,
(back to the whorish party
where piss-coloured pride
is raised to the skies)
while glass smacks against glass
in a cacophony of class,
(a bow to the numb

whose drink made them come)
to the realization that their station
is no more than inebriation,
so in it they live
and give only motive
to raise another,
(against liver and lover,)
'til withered, uncovered,
the desire to touch her
is masked in black—
and never intent,
but bent on being seen,
for the party's collective,
and therefore infective—
thus you pair with the rest
and digest the directive
that the thoughts you had had,
no matter how bad,
are a glory compared
to the depth you're impaired,

and when the sun again is lit
you will not rise with it.

Controllable Flesh

I didn't want to be heard,
each word screaming
from seams I didn't wish
to dehisce,
kissing the listless wrists
of the beautiful and bludgeoned,
the twisted, dutiful love
in the corners of a rusted restaurant
or unpaved park path,
their wrath, as soon started
equally departed—
and weak-hearted, I lapsed
back to my prior silence,
restitching where violence
had torn and worn me down
to the nadir of controllable flesh,
that my apologies might go as unheeded as my cries,
and I'd die, undeterred,
for I'd never been heard.

Peace in the Valley

On a Friday night,
I find peace in the valley,
half a mile from the screams
of an unlit alley,
where men of all sickness
and women of age
discredit their demons
in a moon-darkened cage,
professing their love
in impermanent whispers—
he leans down to kiss her;
she decimates his whisper;
the pulse of a bass,
the final regale,
one night in the black
and the second in jail.
Ah, but hell to their laughter
and damn to their games,
for out here in my haven,
I'm safe from their claims.
And I'm safe from their bruises
and safe from their bars,
and most safe from the knowledge
of what it's like to have scars.

The Return of What Was

I am fine,
daily am I fine.
Fingertips pressed to forehead—
spectres slip, restlessly misled,
drawn and whipped in the valour of dread,
a woeful courtship with concepts long since
dead.

And into the valley, I ruminate still,
shaking and breaking and ready to kill,
while faking is slaking the thirst of my gut
by mistaking the aching I've tried to keep shut.

And the harder I barter to silence the wreck,
a non-starter that martyrs and wraps 'round the neck,
what flares, unaware, in a tear in the lies
is the glare of a pair of recalcitrant eyes.

Can these be mine, intertwined with the black,
designed to assign the decline through attack?
And must I lay claim to this game roiled inside
where it maims with no aim, untamed   for I
  never tried?

A Matter of Clout

I slipped in a daze
in the haze of a drink —
all the ways I could stay
by the clink of the sink
as I retch and I pour
all the more while I link
from the sore to the score
I've not settled to think
is the craze of a lie
and a favour for hell,
for I fell
and I fell
and it didn't end well.
And the daze,
as it softened,
still awakened
my coffin
and bade that I sit
'til I'd made
what I'm offed in.
And I made it of pieces
of blood on the floor
to ignore and abhor
the bleak creak of before.
When the floorboards
rot out
from a sink full of waste,
can I doubt that my clout
was a matter of taste?

And that taste was a lie
and the drink was a crutch,
but to fall was to die,
so,

I died of too much.

Creative Peril

My mind creates unwelcome thoughts
and I must kill them by glass of any kind
that I may persist with what is and desist with what's
    not,
for what is is all well and what's not may unwind

myself from myself, where myself becomes two,
each one strange to the other, as they to themselves
    are,
and they fear what they've done although none of
    them do,
and lost in that wonder, asunder, go far

from the place they were safe, though they made it a
    Hell,
seeing not their blood as cold when a Hell would be
    hot,
and they called themselves sick even though they
    were well,
for they thought they knew all when in fact they knew
    not.

And thus is my station divided in parts,
that that glass may still numb to invite the two back,
and finally forgetting the fictions of their heart,
they return to be one until, with the glass, they crack.

When I destroy the vicious pieces of me,

they lodge in my skin like shrapnel
and burrow deeper and deeper
until they've pierced my heart
and bled me out, although
no one can tell

When I let those vicious pieces live,
they follow me in gratitude,
thanking me with unkindly touches
and reminders that they are my
king, queen, and court jester, alike,
but I must never tell

A Glow-In-The-Dark Raincloud

I'm efficient and deficient,
ambitious, but suspicious
of every beautiful possibility
that threatens me with reality,
for I can't believe in anything
but enmity and grief,
dissociative grief
that blinds me
and bludgeons me
and renders me half of what I want to be.
So I cover my head with the sheets
and try to breathe
hot, viscous air,
as I lay myself bare
to love and death and the impermanence of my share
of Earth's perpetual despair.
And my mother, she tells me,
she yells at me to see
anything but the piece of desperate self-flagellation I
    aspire to be.
So I tell her I'm a rain cloud,
shrouded in rain,
and if she wishes to avoid my pain
and the deep chasms she finds frightening
she'd be best to avoid my lightning
and it's indiscriminate striking.
But instead of contest,
she tells me to rest—
I'm being too loud

and the storm ought to split.
Yes, my mother tells me to be a glow-in-the-dark
    raincloud.
And that's life. That's all there is to it.

Until Collapse

My throat is dry from weeping,
cracked from retching,
lumped from loss,
and silent from absence.

No bottles enough distract,
the concept contracts,
the perception slacks,
the rest revert back,
and that which perverts tracks its coil—sleek and
    undiscerning—across the black

No bottles enough
to replace the absent.
Still, yet another sip
placates the ailing tract.

Corporeal Revolution

My body doesn't work for me,
it's subject to my brain.
My brain has never listened
or enjoys the lie of pain.

My heart won't beat consistent drums,
to hollow stomach songs,
for butterflies have nested there.
(They've lived there all along.)

But I've not lived, for I cannot
create a path in dark
and eyes won't see 'neath bleak beliefs
and hope that never sparks.

Whatever this pain is,

it can't be defined.
It was born in the knots
of the ropes of the mind,
and forever they tighten
to make the pain more,
contesting the senses
too unwell for the war.

This pain is whatever
is left of the hope
that threatens the neck
with the unfurling rope.

Drunken Night Walks

This hallway reminds me of drunken night walks
home after a party or a bar hop or a date or a talk or a
    chance to be friends or a chance to be more or a
    happiest game or a loathsomest bore.
The hum of the lights, a bit white, a bit pink, a bit
    harsh on the eyes, as you try not to think
and the jumble of carpet, brown and marked with a
    streak, that turns straight into wavy and strong into
    weak.
At the end is a window, and at night it's a mirror
of black, and a glare of mistakes, too unclear.
And the door will not open—
the night will not end—
and the morning arrives
as a backhanded friend.
And when next in that hallway, a moment in health,
I'll remember the drunk walk
and I'll remember nothing else.

Interlude I: Love

Involuntary

I haven't taken a breath in...
a real deep breath since...
it's been so long,
the oxygen flow to my brain is gone
and it's impossible to convince
myself that, somehow, I'm still breathing.

"I wish you all the best,"

reads the letter in my hand,
speak the words across your lips,
always grand amongst the damned.

Say my name once more
before you put my kiss to rest
for the bulk of your forever
on the fable of regret.

Does it make your tongue taste fire?
For very soon the smoke will pass,
and the pastures of tomorrow
will be sodded brown with grass.

And to you, my love declining,
lost not in spite of early tells:
I—*I* wish you half the best;
the rest is for someone else.

Lost Her Lie

In an ear or under thunder
with a soul yet cast asunder
in the blunder of a midnight wreck of doubt,

her sweet insanity rolled on
as rain rolled off the breath at dawn
of death prolonged, a candle never to burn out.

For she had lived as she had lost
and never could assign the cost
for what she'd done and what she'd killed and what
she'd been,

as she was nothing for a man
to understand amongst the damned,
though, in her mind, her mind was buried past her
key.

And she was free, a libertine,
a queen of dreams, the world unseen,
and past the shroud of her misfortune
lay her right.

And she was free, as she had been
since she had learned to drop the screen
that made her growth seem gloom,
and day a paltry night.

But I saw through,

I always knew,
yet still I fell
upon my knees

for, though I saw,
it was too raw
to be believed.

And I could sense
that far below
there was a girl
I'd never know

although I'd met her
in a haze,
lost and bereaved.

Recalcitrant and ignorant
yet alluring, young, and coy.
Did she know me as a man
or just recall me as a boy?

Though it's been a thousand years,
I saw the woman in her eye.
Immortal truth beneath the shield
and the impertinence to try
to break a path through what she was,
although it made a good man cry,
so, I shook when I discovered
that at 8:14 tonight she lost her lie.

And the world that curled

about us twirled and hurled
itself away.

And the life we knew
and grew that flew
us from our sordid day

was awash with loss,
embossed in gloss
that crossed all sense of time.

For, past the laughs
and halves
and traps
and scraps
we lived and loved that lie.

Headstrong, stubborn, vicious,
a vivacious, precious fool,
did she know that she was transient
or weep as she unspooled?

Though the ages passed by dazedly,
I could tell what she possessed.
But eternal lack of satiety
was the burden in her chest.
And hearts and souls that she consumed
were ever deferent to her best
for it was a sin, beneath her innocence,
to ignore her soft behest.

So, what a world rotates about me

if the impossible is nigh?
If the tremors shake foundations
mustn't all who topple die?
This is no life, this is no sanctum
if laws that govern won't apply,
as what she drew designed existence,
yet at 8:14 tonight, she lost her lie.

You must have scars—

don't let me see;
it makes me sick
when I believe
that others' pain
approaches mine.
For me to suffer,
you must be fine.

i. In Heat

A piece of me went missing
on the desert of your tongue,
where I traipsed on ancient sands
in wanton days when I was young;
those days you taught me to endure
the bleak intensity of heat
until I found myself unsure,
and in the dehydration weak;
those days you built me from the grains,
all resurrected 'fore the storm,
before inflicted by that pain
I learned to cower 'neath the warm;
those days are left but ne'er forgotten,
though in my fading are so old,
I learned to love what I had gotten,
but that, love, I much prefer the cold.

ii. In Retreat

A piece of me went missing
on the arctic of your neck,
where I slipped off glistening glaciers
on halcyon days in youthful wreck;
those days you taught me to revert
to a fetal bundle in the chill
until I found myself unnerved
and in the depths, inspired to kill;
those days you built me from the snow,
struck coal my eyes before the frost
until my burden came to grow—
I learned to live before I lost;
those days, they threaten to return,
though I have spurned what once I felt,
and while I tried to love the burn,
I couldn't help it, love, but melt.

iii. In Deceit

A piece of me went missing
in the void beneath your breast,
where I shuttled through the darkness,
seeking life, but finding rest;
those days you taught me to be humble,
not to assume, believe, expect,
until, in absence, I had bumbled
all about the vacant trek;
those days you scattered me in atoms
before the nucleus could die
that when I reached life's final stratum
I might relinquish faith and cry;
those days continue to the present,
if there's a present left to grieve.
I try to love the nothing, pleasant,
but, love, despite you, I believe.

But I Miss You

Hello love,
I miss you;
I'm not in love with you,
but I miss you;
I don't need your body,
but I miss you;
I don't need your reciprocation,
but I'd appreciate it—
just a little bit,
the thought you at least remember me,
have time to spend with me,
like we may ever be,
again, momentarily
a tiny piece of that infinite life
that pauses,
just for a moment,
to remember our shared time.

Passing Through (or, the Fury of the Mundane)

Here, we are all but passersby,
akin for difference made,
by the panoply of fires
from the asphalt 'gainst the tires,
which, a lover of the rubber,
lets one pass, while still it stays.
And in the night when all is quiet
And a headlight splits the black,
it will hold the scraps of metal,
fading friends whose love will settle
but a moment, 'til the pedal
draws the fleeting meeting secret,
though remembered in the cracks.
At least something loves the traveller,
for they, each other, often spurn,
gifts of fingers and of curses
left to linger 'til the hearses
can collect what they detect,
wrought of speed perceived as valour,
soon the nurse of siblings' pallor,
for though they're one, each never learns.

Projected Faces

I know you have a beautiful soul,
but stripped to your bones
I still can't find it.
I'd swear it's there,
I can feel it pulsing,
or is that just the wish
of my weak heart convulsing?

She led with the predisposition

of deliberation,
a sickly fine jest
balanced on the kiss of inebriation
and the invalidation
of the night previous' mess,
lest it be said
that there is meaning in the unmeaning fog
that defines the disbelieving slog
between tepid sexual deliverance and indifference,
the acceptance I expected
and the organs she dissected
with just a few solemn words
of retraction,
the depreciation of a dissatisfied impression.
But at least that brief night's distraction
was wrought of a beautiful direction,
irrespective of the laughter
that would never come thereafter.

Tactile Lies

I long for
summers
made of sweat
from pores
my body
never met
within the arms
of heat and love,
in tactile lies
and harms thereof.

Once More

If you are to come,
please come lightly
for I fear I cannot bear the burn
of a thousand eyelash lashes
on a stomach overturned
by every here and there decision,
some of mine and some of yours,
that wreak division on my vision
and rescission on my mores.
For when I spoke,
I spoke with caution,
on the fear that you might crack,
and as you watched I botched the option
that I might ever take it back.
Thus, now, I ask
without restriction,
that you might moderate your track,
for though fault came by my infliction,
still, I wish we could go back.

Gone with the Flow

You were like the ocean,
crashing down on me
and whisking me away
to where no one else could see.

You were like the ocean,
you took me for a ride.
And, when finally I was stranded there,
you waved and passed me by.

Perfection, in the arms of a stranger

The future contained not you,
not in the certitude I knew to be true,
that I drew upon the pitted canvas
in straight lines, intertwined alone
by the notion that every emotion
I'd deigned to endure was linear
and purposed well beyond the surface,
that being nervous had been worth it
for some defined design I could find and rewind over
and again in my mind—
that this one or that, tangible for presence,
yet intangible in essence,
should ensue to imbue
upon the new some provision
of precision, a mission aligned
with a vision, a reason
to seize on, to please,
drawn by daggers of patience and hope,
unambiguously, to cope
with the tamped down realizations
of pointlessly pointed expectations,
marked with striations of considered inflation
of tomorrows decided,
invited and lighted down paths undivided,
cast in the wrath of a whirlpool
that spits true, straight to you,
through tributaries and misdirections,

momentarily buried, but thereafter protected,
selecting from kismet and predestination
the conflation of aberrations,
set and reset to refine expectations;
and after the blind,
no more trapped by the line,
the cold vision beyond
the decision of revision
will hold that you're gone;
and off and on
I must scoff as I spawn
increasing derision,
self-sought for the thoughts
that caught in my histories,
blistering mysteries
in fictitious resolve
I believed could be solved,
for my certitude caused,
paused, and selected
a future directed
but reality elected,
beyond my mind's blind demand—
it can follow no guide,
for buried inside,
there is nothing to find
or ever rewind,
as the path I thought for her,
was truly disorder,
and I've merely been trapped for
the thought I could have her
and thus, memory full,
so shall I be pulled

from time immemorial
until time ever after.

Now and End

Kiss me eternally
until eternity turns its back on me
and leaves me at the end
that is the present
bearing down on me,
the unpleasant seed
still growing
despite the cultivated enmity
within now and then's
conspiracy
to create the will
that will never be.

Adieu

I wish you well in your absence,
that you may flout despair
and care, alone, for the burgeoning sea
that swirls in decadence.

And may those waters breathe calm
to ebb and flow
that you may go liltingly free
and declare loves with aplomb.

And may those loves unsaved,
led seaward by false design,
realign from your fleeting fancy,
and tuck your head beneath the waves.

Interlude II: Hate

Inside Myself

All alone, I sink inside myself
and find there's nothing there.
I tried to give you everything,
but nothing can't be shared.

Re-Play

I've been playing this…
I don't know,
would you call it a game
when all the moves are destined
and the outcome is the same?
And the pieces look like people,
just a plastic you and me,
melted down to bastard fragments
that subsist on agony.
This game, it isn't fun,
yet it starts and starts again—
it's not the fact that I've been losing,
it's that no one ever wins.

Several Years Dead

I was 17
I was 17

as we all have been
save for those still yet to be,
those who don't know what it means

to be old at 17

a meek, half-faded dream

to be old at 17.

Today I Am

I looked in the mirror and saw myself as a man
for the first time,
with a beard and trimmed cut,
with all the pieces of what
I imagine must lurk beneath the skin
of other men, that then burrow in
to the very processes of their existence
and burst forth, between cowardice and reticence,
to present a final, stunted product in the infinite
    assembly line.
And now, finally, it is my time.

Dissociation

My walls are hung with paintings
for the white craves some design,
and while sublimely it may peacock
what a pity it's not mine.
No, I claimed them from an artist
whose expertise was in the soul,
and so coldly did I suffer
as I swallowed his, quite whole.
Now his mind is sprayed 'cross frames
while his body is in bed,
and he said "O what a shame
that to be great I must be dead!"
And I apologized for crudeness,
for I hate to be so terse,
"but though the curse of shaded life is sad
to be forgot in death is worse."
He replied, "but if you take what's mine
I won't be gone at all!"
So, I call this my defence
and tell the lie, "These are my walls."

Good Evening, Absence

Your fledgling soul,
cold, unrolled, edging bold,
eventually sold for fool's gold.
Ostensibly lost from the light,
embossed in the night
clouds, bleak black on black,
inviting rain, loud, yet weak:
effervescent acid attacks and cracks
dusty pavement, incessant, until,
acquiescent, it melts back, placid,
and is filled, iridescent, 'til killed
and spilled—uncaring, unwilled—
thrust asunder, blundering the broken hold,
untold—that soul, in thunder shaking,
breaking and defeated
'til the purchase, awakening, is completed.

The Tattoo Fades

I felt this x etch itself into my skin
in black and vermilion—
willing itself to become part of my body
while, simultaneously, it carved me away
and left the billion pieces that were me,
or were the concept of me,
under a morose, starry infinity,
dripping with serenity
in its slow demise—
all of us dragged together
to eternity.
But, in the interim, why don't you burn with me?
The fire is freshly lit
and every piece of me that falls into it
is just another cheer for a bygone year
in the indifference of dear, dear time.

Lost Mornings

I made the mistake
of letting the rain
wash the beauty away
instead of trying to tell
what beauty there was
in the way that the water fell.

Reflections of Yesterday

I knew the day
I heard my name
when I was all alone
and felt it strange
and felt it wrong
to find myself
in my own brain
was the day I had to change

(to what?)

I had to change

and, in this knowledge, I found peace
that I had changed

(though I had not)

and, in this ignorance, I found peace
that I had changed

And Suddenly...

One.

Moment.

No precursor borne
nor expectation built;
nonetheless, permanence,
unassuageable guilt.
The reparation's will,
blown asunder in trumpets
laid with rusted brass
which tear the mass,
and what was before,
wrought from eons,
weathered and aged as stone,
is sliced flesh from flesh
as tenderly as if
sweet and unknown.

And soon stitches may cross
to bind the parts,
so bleakly flapping free.
But through thread so thin,
inevitably,
still the wound can see.

To Live

The cold of my directive,
issued rough and introspective,
while the hold is ineffective
yet enough, from my perspective.
Hell, I know that I'm defective,
constant negative selective,
bent to flow from the collective—
to a speculative objective—
strewn and bloomed to be connective
but invariably prospective,
ever doomed to be reflective,
and terribly self-invective.
Tainted placation too protective,
for it's shamefully infective,
and the station claims corrective,
but absent games: O so subjective.

That Crowded Death

I fear for you,
my love and well.
If gone, I'll bide
my time in Hell.
If gone, I'll breathe
in counting breaths
'til I can join
that crowded death.

Stop to Smell the Roses Overhead

I rushed
so fast
I couldn't see
the world passing by,
forgetting me.

Interlude III: Death

54

The Waking Dream

The ghost who lives within this flesh,
he knows he's never seen.

His mind repugnant, cruelty fresh,
he haunts the waking dream.

A Light That Never Glows

When I woke up
and that feeling was gone,
I didn't know how to feel anything anymore—
when so long it went on and on
until it consumed me
and I consumed it back
in a cycle we knew
but didn't know what for.

When it fell
then we fell,
'til I wasted away,
and I swelled
from the shell
too unwell
to behave
in the way
that my mind
(is it mine)
would desire.
And the liar
in my fall's
only truth
was inspired

by what it had made in the midst of this sick
and it had made me
but said I had made it.

And it burrowed inside,
like a worm under skin
struck with knives that pulled out
but that never went in
and that hovered like angels
who never knew God
but had once vaguely heard
that their wings were a fraud;
and they tittered and teased
and they promised their dark,
but when dark lives inside
then they don't leave a mark.

So, forever they stay
'til the day I awake
and, the broken bits dead,
I feel certain I'll break.
But the fear, now erased,
how I fear now to lose
as it grows and it flows
but, unable to choose,
it just goes
and it goes
and it goes
and it goes,
down and more down yet it slows,   slows,
          slows:

in the absence of dark,
a light that never glows.

Inaction

They watched each other as they lost themselves.
They watched each other fall to someone else.
They watched each other do their best to change.
They watched each other become something strange.
They watched each other war with their confusion.
They watched each other accept a new delusion.
They watched each other, sure they'd be forever okay.
They watched each other slowly fade away.

Nesting Lives

Behind the door stood a child,
behind the child stood a man,
behind the man stood the world,
behind the world stood our plans,

behind our plans fell our hope,
behind our hope fell our love,
behind our love fell our need,
and looking down from up above

it all seemed so small,
like life had never happened at all.

Distant Lights

Foul, horrid, yet florid distraction,
father to failure and son of inaction.
Brazen and crazy, resultantly lazy:
the hours spent in waste are empowered to faze me
and daily, assail me, 'til broken and palely
I scream for the dream as apathy derails me.
While beaten, half-eaten, and tauntingly present
desires misfired inspire cold lament:
"O what have I done when the fun's abolition
of all that I call for, my falling ambition!
I've lost—at what cost!—and been tossed aside,
meek,
left to wail and to flail; in catastrophe's bleak
and dark middle I fiddled in whittling rhymes,
until lowly and slowly I ran out of time!"

Back and Forth and Back

My head is dying
is dying
is dying.

Yet my body is standing,
unendingly landing
on soles undermining,
assigning, designing,
floating wherever,
yet never exploding,
in spite of the goading
that one may dissever
its line from declining;
for as one, misaligning,
will decay, notwithstanding
incessant commanding.

Lying is
Lying is
Lying is my dread.

Songs of Burden

The music
made me
dance inside,
pallid skin
that nearly
died;
whispered
lyrics
never stayed,
songs of burden
never played.

In Relief

Where the knees buckle
and muscle loses shape,
its elastic bands snapping
the skin to the ground,

so far down
from that perch
where the stomach lurched
at every sound

and the chest fluttered,
not with butterflies,
but with lies told to the self
in staccato stutters,

the soul soured
and gracelessly deflowered
by the threat of
unavoidable grief

so soon, so gone
in the shadow of relief,
so hidden in darkness,
is unable to speak

until our belief
that there is no relief
exacerbates lies
and lulls truth to sleep.

Dust of the Iris

I didn't mean to step on
the dead irises
that once sprouted out between
the crevices in the road;
and I never wanted to break up
the fractured asphalt
that I paved over years of
dust and faded trails;
and the dust is my memories,
and the trails are the histories
of a billion upon billions
of half-naked ancestries,
who walked where I may drive
and who died that I may be alive—
but those irises,
meant ever to last
are now dead, and dead again,
for my unwitting ill-deed,
and my future is but their past.

Try Again

Blood, blood bludgeoned enough
What humour carved my tongue this rough?
Smiling, beguiling, ever-smitten
A laughless ode of solemn stuff,
It's hard to read when nothing's written.

I drew on the scars, circumspect,
just to see if they'd infect
and waltz me to the end of men
that I could resurrect
to do it yet again.

Now wrap me up warm and clean,
bereft and left and ne'ermore seen
as I float the rapids, drenched in doubt,
the darkest vessel in the ravine,
wailing to be carried out.

My Only Consistency

What death has befallen the scores of men and
　　women I have adored and given the depths of my
　　being, though they see not the mask I hold—
For I have given them the black pieces along with the
　　gold, and commanded them rudely, by my
presumption, to give a damn; and they do, through
　　and through.
So in the absence of their touch and humanity—the
　　essence of continuity they breed and proffer—I
　　offer the only explanation I can fathom, in the
　　darkest chasm of a miswired mentality, marred by
　　a duality of sanity and depravity, which is that they
　　must be dead.
Return them please! afford some sign of life in those I
　　need, those who hold the pieces I entrusted, those
　　for whom I've lusted with asexual desire, whose
　　mere presence raises me and whose touch lifts me
　　higher...
And every time—for there are so many times—and
　　infinitely without rhyme, yet infinitely infiltrating
　　my mind, assurance comes and critiques the lie
　　that blindly my head has recreated. Over and over
　　again.
For I know not how to live without this curiosity
　　looming over me; and every temporary anxiety is
　　washed away inevitably, but those that renew,
　　though persistently untrue, persevere to haunt
　　freely.
And thus, it is those who know whom I fear will go,

by means I cannot control or slow, and leave me
with the perpetual fear, indefinitely, as my only
true consistency.

The Acquisition of a Dream

And if you are to discover silence,
then you may name it.

And you may name it for the roses,
or you may name it for the bastions,
or you may name it for the patience,
or you may not name it at all.

But if you choose not to name it,
recall what you have relinquished before
and consider the increasing menagerie
of dead ideas and transitory thoughts,

the broken inklings and the metastasized failures,
every vow of fickle fancy,
every intended ride upon the starlight
that concluded an inch from the atmosphere.

And wonder whether you are worthy of the silence at
    all,
or if, rather, the silence has already named you.

Gone and Gone Again

Entrenched within
ceaseless distance,
fingers grasping as for clouds,
sweat, pungent, staining crooked fingers
that yearn
for full extent, yet know,
even in the loudest moments
and brightest despairs,
that lengths yet so long
nonetheless will remain unbreachable,
and resultantly unreached,
shrivel about the deceptive nothing
until desperate hands fold in upon themselves—
the crack of bones for cold company—
in a cruel, fragile self-embrace.

Erosion

Ignore my scarred countenance,
where pieces of flesh, like marble from antiquity,
cut ever to last
are cut greater by counting,
which is seldom more looked upon,
save in reflection,
and even then met by wincing.
Meaning is long lost in the lines
and their lessons departed with time.
And the remains are only worth seeing
by those who seek reminder
not to squander
their capable being.
For the minutes to come
soon will mingle
with those we know,
have known,
and used to know.
And then what?

Morning Whispers

Awake at night
and dead by day,
infinitely
in decay—
morning whispers
in the way.

Self-Revitalization

There was a time
when I was gone,
a piece of dust
floating on,

but in return
uninjured yet,
I reach whatever
peak I'll get.

Slow suicide

Thin in the House of the Lord,
in the house of absurd,
I'm alive
and I'm sure
I'm alive
and I'm sure
I'm alive
and I'm sure
I'm alive.
If I die,
I won't know
what I'm doing—
Oh I—
Oh I—
in the tourniquet
bound 'round my neck,
I'm alive in the sex
of my mind—
I'm a wreck
in the bleeding, believing
to unwind
in the trek
of a mind
too bereft
to be fine
'round the neck
I shall wind and I'll wind and I'll wind 'til I die,
'cause reality's hell
and this hell is a lie.

Even hell is a lie,
yet I try and I try—
an insanity by
passing by, passing by, passing by
the insanity
of my calamity
half inanity—
all of my soul
enduring banality,
half of reality,
quarter of malady
all of the whole.

Dead in the middle,
I twiddle my thumbs,
awaiting the victual
of all the above,
and what in the world
do I mean when I mean that I'm mean
and I've seen
the un-been,
the unmaimed,
the un-been,
the unmaimed,
the unseen,
the untamed—
I'm half of myself
and I'm all the deranged
and the nonsense I've conquered
is half of the game
that I've played
in this life,

though this life
is the same.

The game of this life
that I've lived
and I've died,
and already I've given
the bulk of my time,
and the rest I have given
to the test of my crimes,
and I've failed even those
thus, I've fully maligned—

thus, I've fully maligned
every time
I've been blind
and been blinded by hope
in the slow suicide
we call life,
we call time,
we call all we've aligned.
Though we bleed out our souls
and design our decline
De
cline
De
Cl
Ine
De
C
L
I

N
E
to define.

To define what we know,
we must grow from our grind
into powder and rust,
yes, we must,
hell, we must;
in divinity's trust,
we are thrust
into dust.

Slow, slow suicide
what it is
is a life.
What it is,
yes, I might.
What it is,
yes, I die.
What it is,
no, a life.
Why oh why
can I try
but can never refine
in myself, in my lies, in the vacuum of time
in myself, in my lies, in the vacuum of time
in the malarkey waiting
at the end of the line.
I don't know, I don't know,
oh my hell, I don't know
where I go when I go to the end of my soul.

Can I live in a world where my soul is a joke,
where the joke of the world
is the gag of a choke
of a breath of a gasp
of a shot in the neck
of a knife to the heart
and a heart to my sex?
And my sex to the point
that a point can be bent
and the bend of a tongue
in the ear of a wreck
in the pull of a gravity
made from a peck
on the cheek
from an amity
born from a beck
and a call
and a fall
and the gall
of a world
that can kill any man
and can kill any girl
and can sling the exalted by neck or by toe
and can murder a lover
in desolate glow?

This, the power of evil
the children of greed,
is a world without love
without hate
without need.

I don't need you,
you bastard,
you hater of God.
I don't need you to tell me
my life's a façade.
I don't need you,
you bitchwhore,
you murdering cad.
Your abhorrence is wanting,
too good to be bad.
But you want to be evil,
you think you've got grit,
you don't know you're a prophet
of ineloquent wit.
I don't need you,
you blackguard,
you've done what you can.
I can't kill you,
you blackguard,
but my innocence can.

Though it died long ago,
so I think it was fake,
just a vision of angels
my love may forsake
in its quest for abandon—
it abandons me still—
and what we may sequester
from hell
in our will.

In the seasons of love
and the breadth of decay,
they fall anyway
how they fall,
anyway.
Watch them bleed and untether
from all that we knew.
Slow suicide, slow suicide,
a life too untrue.
Slow suicide, slow suicide
a life we unknew,
much too true to be prosperous,
much too false to be new,
much too new to be real
much too real to undo,
much too real to be lie,
much too false to be specious,
much too specious to try,
much too live to be worthless,
much too sex to be love,
much too love to be sex,
and the middle of all
is the subtext of next.
And the next that we lived in,
the next we revealed,
an orphan of love
and a hanged man of zeal.

And the next that we lived in
was unlived and killed,
as frank as we were
in unlimited will.

And the next that we lived in
was sex and despair,
and despair and unliving
and death
everywhere.

A pause in the worthless;
a pause in the pain;
a pause in the bullet
interred in my brain.
A pause in the wanton
regret of a life
I chose not to live

kill 'em all 'til we die.

"You're a worthless twit"
I'm a worthless twit.
I've heard it all
and I'm tired of the bit
and the piece
and the peace
and the lease
on a life
I've been told it's a sin
if I must sacrifice.
Never asked,
never wanted,
but perilously told,
with no love
I'm a ruin,
with no warmth

I am cold.

Didn't choose to be cold;
didn't choose to be loved;
didn't choose to be ruined
or the outcomes thereof;
didn't choose to be needed,
yet need me, you do;
didn't choose to be heeded;
you don't see it through.

I'm a piece of the puzzle, a puzzle you made.
But you stole all the pieces
and bade that I stay;
though so staid, I accomplished
what little you frayed,
and though life is a death,
still, in death, I'm waylaid
into life,
into living
the virulent cure,
the loss of an icon,
the victory pure

in a slow, slow suicide
too quick to be real,
an attrition to dust,
a perdition of zeal.

So alive,
yet so dead,
from the moment of birth

we arrive
at the head
of a humourless mirth
where we laugh
and we laugh
and we laugh
'til we die,
and the shortness of breath
may yet cure the divide
between life
and the pain
we endure,
that we live,
though we hate
to survive
this irate,
yet we live.

Slow, slow suicide
from birth
to dust
to air,
we give ourselves
to the atmosphere
but NOTHING
(nothing)
cares.

Epilogue

)

I listen to this music
to drown out the sound
of the record in my head
that never rhymes
and never flows
or glows
(it grows)
and goes
around and 'round and 'round
and scratches, sticks
with vicious clicks
(aroun-shh 'roun-shh 'roun-shh...

O, this feeble goodbye:

though again we may...nay, will
connect,
that hours dithering, overtured in sentiment and
woven in gleesome tears, more further spent—
as russet in autumn 'pon tepid dew—
shall in twine persist.

The immediate.
The recognition.
The vulgar separation.

Now, my loves, we're strangers.